W9-BBC-397

A Great Idea

Hybrid Cars

by Bonnie Juettner

NORWOOD HOUSE PRESS

Norwood House Press
PO Box 316598
Chicago, Illinois 60631

For information regarding Norwood House Press, please visit our Web site at:

www.norwoodhousepress.com or call 866-565-2900.

LIBRARY OF CONGRESS CATALOGING-IN-PUBLICATION DATA

Juettner, Bonnie.
  Hybrid cars / by Bonnie Juettner.
     p. cm. —(A great idea)
  Includes bibliographical references.
  Summary: "Describes the invention and development of hybrid cars. Includes
glossary, Web sites, and bibliography for further reading"—Provided by publisher.
  ISBN-13: 978-1-59953-193-9 (library edition : alk. paper)
  ISBN-10: 1-59953-193-3 (library edition : alk. paper)
 1. Hybrid electric cars—Juvenile literature. I. Title.
  TL221.15.J84 2009
  629.22'93—dc22

                                                         2008022970

Manufactured in the United States of America in North Mankato, Minnesota
153R-022010

Contents

Chapter 1:
The Energy Crisis
4

Chapter 2:
Developing Hybrid Cars
13

Chapter 3:
Changing the History of Automaking
21

Chapter 4:
What's Next?
32

Glossary
43

For More Information
45

Index
47

Picture Credits
48

About the Author
48

Note: Words that are **bolded** in the text are defined in the glossary on page 43.

The Energy Crisis

"I'm sorry, lady, but you can't butt in line like that. We'll have a riot on our hands," said the gas station attendant. The year was 1979, and the woman just wanted to fill her car's gas tank. But she hadn't noticed the long line of cars that was stretching down the street.

In 1973 and 1974, and again in 1979, cars and trucks often had to line up at gas stations. Some of the lines were a mile (1.6km) long. Drivers had to wait for as long as two hours. Cars and trucks with odd-numbered license plates could buy gas on odd-numbered days. Cars and trucks with even-numbered license plates could buy gas on even-numbered days. Some states had a flag system. A green flag meant that anyone could buy gas. A yellow flag meant that only cars and trucks with the right kind of license plate number—odd or even—for that day

Cars line up for blocks as drivers wait to fill up their tanks during the 1970s energy crisis.

A Scarce Resource

Politics caused the gasoline crisis in the 1970s. Gasoline, or gas for short, is made from a type of oil. This oil is a **fossil fuel** that comes from deep below the Earth's surface. Once taken from the Earth it can be **refined** and made into gasoline. In the 1970s, the countries that produced the most oil decided to sell less of it to the United States. However, today most experts think that we will eventually run out of oil from fossil fuels.

Right now Earth still has oil for the world's cars, trucks, trains, ships, and

could buy gas. A red flag meant the station did not have any gas to sell.

Sometimes, gas stations could not allow drivers to fill their tanks. They could have only a small ration of gas. "I had one woman that told me to find her another job," said Ronald Hartman, the manager of a Pennsylvania gas station. "I sold her ten dollars worth of gas and she said that wouldn't get her to work."

airplanes. The supply of fossil fuels is uncertain, though. As a result, they have become very expensive. In 2008 drivers did not have to wait in line to fill their tanks, but they had to pay more than four dollars a gallon (3.78L) for it. (In 1978 gas cost about 65 cents a gallon.) Nobody can be certain how long fossil fuels will last. It depends, in part, on whether people discover more in places where it has never been mined before. It also depends on whether inventors figure out ways to take more oil out of natural **reserves**. For example, inventors might find ways to take out more oil from reserves that have been abandoned. They might find ways to pump oil out of **oil shale**.

The lack of fossil fuels has everyone worried. It makes airplane flights a lot more expensive. Food gets more expensive because truckers need to spend more money on fuel to get food to stores. In poor countries the price of food is even more of a concern. What will we do?

Throughout history, people have solved problems by inventing new technologies.

How Long Will Earth's Oil Last?

Nobody is certain how long Earth's oil will last. However, many scientists have tried to guess. Scientists at the Association for the Study of Peak Oil predict that oil production will stop increasing. At that point, they think oil production will start to decline, or slow down. In 2004 physicist Kjell Aleklett imagined a glass that held all the oil the world was using in a year. He said the world had consumed 36 glasses of oil since oil was first discovered. Also, he estimated, there were somewhere between 36 and 40 glasses of oil left in oil reserves. Oil reserves contain oil that has been discovered but has not yet been pumped.

But we also know there is oil in the world that has not yet been discovered. Aleklett hypothesized that the equivalent of 12 more glasses of oil might still be out there, waiting to be discovered. Other scientists disagree. Some think there is more. They think that the equivalent of 20 or 24 glasses of oil still remains undiscovered.

There is one more thing that makes it hard to predict how long oil will last. Each year, the world uses more oil than it did the year before. Aleklett's glasses of oil are the equivalent of one year of oil use—but only if the year is 2004. Each year since then the world has used a glass of oil—and then some. As countries such as China develop manufacturing industries, the demand for oil will go up. The world will use more oil each year.

Although scientists do not agree about when the oil will run out, they are sure of one thing. Oil is a nonrenewable resource. Sooner or later there will be none left.

This is happening with cars. Carmakers know they have to come up with solutions. In the future, if cars are only able to run on gasoline, only wealthy people will be able to drive. Others will start to take the bus or walk or ride bicycles. Carmakers could go out of business. So they have begun to consider alternative technologies instead.

Electric Cars

Inventors wanted to come up with a car that didn't have to use fossil fuel. They experimented with **electric cars**. Surprisingly, this was an old technology. Your great grandparents may have had an electric car! The first electric car was developed at the same time as the gasoline car, in the late 1800s.

At the beginning of the 20th century, when people first began to buy cars, electric cars sold better than gasoline cars. In 1897 New York City had a fleet of electric taxis. Why? In the early 1900s, gasoline cars were smelly, noisy, and bumpy to ride

Did You Know?

You could buy more with a dollar in 1978 than you can today. Over time, prices tend to go up. This is called inflation. To buy the same amount of food (or gas) that a dollar would buy in 1978, you would need a little more than three dollars today.

in. Electric cars were much quieter and more peaceful. But electric cars could not drive very far or go very fast. One popular electric car, the 1902 Phaeton, had a top speed of 14 miles (22.5km) per hour. It could only go 18 miles (28.9km) before it had to **recharge**.

In the 1920s gasoline cars began to out-sell electric cars. Gasoline cars were still smelly and noisy, but they could travel long distances. Electric cars worked well for driving short distances in cities. In the 1920s the United States began to build more roads connecting cities and leading to interesting places, like national parks. People wanted to take road trips, and that meant they wanted gasoline engines. Recharging an electric battery was difficult and would make the trip even longer.

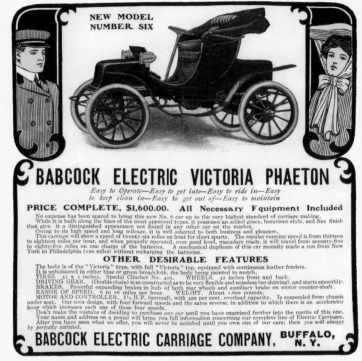

An old advertisement promotes the electric Phaeton car, whose top speed was 14 miles (22.5km) per hour.

In the 1970s, with the gas shortage, inventors began to think about electric cars again. Some inventors replaced gasoline engines with electric batteries. Some

Did You Know?

In the 1950s and 1960s American cars were getting bigger and bigger. Foreign cars were smaller. But the gas crisis of the 1970s spurred Americans to buy compact cars from other countries. One of the first compact cars to become a hit in the United States was the 1976 Honda Accord.

Solectria Corporation converted Geo Metro sedans. The electric Geo Metros could usually drive about 50 miles (80.4km) before recharging.

One electric Geo Metro, however, managed to drive more than 200 miles (321.8km) on a single charge. It was competing in the American Tour de Sol—a yearly electric vehicle competition.

Car manufacturers began to design their own electric cars. In the early 1990s Ford

Solectria converted gasoline engines to electric motors. One of the company's motors is shown.

companies specialized in electric car conversions. U.S. Electricar specialized in converting Chevrolet S-10 pickup trucks. The converted trucks could drive 60 miles (96.5km) before they had to be recharged.

The EV Challenge

Since 1995, middle and high school students have helped to design alternative cars. In 1995 the Caroline Electric Vehicle Coalition (CEVC) began to hold a yearly contest. High school students designed and built electric cars that would be legal to drive on the street, or they converted existing cars by replacing gasoline engines with electric batteries. At first the students were required to build electric cars. But in 2007 CEVC changed the name of the challenge to SMARTT. The new name stood for Students Making Advancements in Renewable Transportation Technology. The SMARTT challenge is slightly different from the EV challenge. Students no longer had to build electric cars. If they chose to, they could build cars that used alternative fuels instead.

Middle school students participate in the challenge, too. But they build model cars. Model cars are much smaller than full-size cars. The middle school students power their cars with photovoltaic solar panels and electric motors. Each car in the middle school challenge, called the Junior Solar Sprint, has to carry a 12-ounce (340.2g) soft drink can as its cargo. The can stands for the weight of passengers and cargo in a full-size car.

High school students take part in an electric vehicle (EV) challenge.

designed the Ecostar. The Ecostar could drive nearly 100 miles (161km) without recharging, at speeds of up to 70 miles (112.6km) per hour. An electric version of the Ford Ranger pickup could travel 65 miles (104.6km), at up to 75 miles (120.7km) per hour. It could accelerate from 0 to 50 miles (0 to 80.4km) per hour in twelve seconds. GM designed the EV1, a two-passenger electric sports car. The EV1 could go from 0 to 50 miles per hour in seven seconds. It could travel 80 miles (128.7km) at speeds up to 80 miles per hour. GM also designed an electric Chevrolet S-10, with a range of 45 miles (72.4km). By 1998 carmakers such as Toyota, Honda, and Chrysler were all selling electric cars.

The electric cars worked well and could drive fast. But they had one big disadvantage. Recharging an electric car could take from seven to twelve hours, depending on the car. In contrast, it only takes a few minutes to refill a gas tank. Also, the new electric cars were expensive—$30,000 to $40,000 in 1998. After about four years, they needed their batteries replaced. The batteries could be expensive, too—about $2,000. Automobile designers needed to find a way to make electric cars as practical to use as cars with gasoline engines. They began to think creatively. What would you get if you crossed a gasoline engine with an electric battery? The result was a car for the 21st century—a **hybrid** car.

Chapter 2

Developing Hybrid Cars

In 1993 cars were back to being "king." Gas cost about half of what it had in 1981. American companies began to concentrate on making large sport utility vehicles (SUVs). SUVs use around twice as much gas to drive the same distance as small compact cars.

But Eiji Toyoda, the chairman of Toyota, was concerned. He knew that oil was a nonrenewable resource. Gas prices could not remain low forever. How would car companies be affected when gas prices began to rise?

Did You Know?

The world uses about 80 million barrels of oil every day.

A Car for the 21st Century

Toyoda wanted to develop a new kind of car and not wait for gas prices to rise again. The new car had to use much less gas. It had to get much better **mileage**. The other executives agreed. Yoshiro Kimbara, the vice president in charge of research and development, started the G21 Project. Kimbara went to Toyota's engineers and gave them their instructions. He wanted a car that would get at least 48 miles (77.2km) per gallon.

At the time, Toyota's most fuel-efficient car was the Corolla. Toyota specialized in making these types of cars, and the Corolla was one of the best in the world. A 1993 Corolla could get about 24 miles (38.6km) per gallon in the city. So Toyota's leaders were asking engineers to design a car that would be twice as efficient as any car they had ever made before.

The Impossible Dream

Toyota put engineer Takeshi Uchiyamada in charge of the design. Uchiyamada's father had been a Toyota engineer. His father had designed the Toyota Crown. As a teenager, Uchiyamada had always wanted to be just like his dad and design a new car. This was his chance. He set to work.

Uchiyamada's first design had a gas engine. He did not build a car based on the first design. But he estimated that it would get 47.5 miles (76.4km) per gallon. It would do what Toyota had asked him to do—improve **fuel efficiency** by 50 percent. Toyota executives were not satisfied.

Early Hybrids

Toyota's engineers were not the first ever to build a hybrid car. Some early carmakers also built hybrids. In 1902 Ferdinand Porsche designed a car with electric motors built into each of the front wheels. In 1905 the F.A. Woods Auto Company designed a one-person car with two engines. One engine burned gasoline. The other used an electric battery. Most of the time drivers would use the electric battery. But if they needed to make a long road trip, they could remove the electric battery and replace it with the gasoline engine. The swapping procedure was supposed to take fifteen minutes.

Drivers didn't like the Woods and Porsche hybrids. Hybrid cars today have computers that tell the car when to switch between gas and electric power. But in the early 1900s, the driver had to do that. As a result, driving early hybrids was complicated and difficult. It took the development of computers to make hybrid cars drivable for everyday use.

This early hybrid vehicle from the 1900s was designed by Ferdinand Porsche.

They wanted a more modern, different car. They wanted a car that people would be awed by. They also wanted a car that would be more imaginative and harder for other car companies to copy.

Toyota's engineers had been experimenting with hybrid engines for years. A hybrid car has both a gasoline engine and an electric battery. It uses electricity as much as possible but can run on gas when it needs to. The engineers believed a hybrid engine was the answer. But they had to convince Toyota leaders that the car would still be affordable.

Finally, everyone at Toyota decided to try the hybrid engine, but they gave engineers a nearly impossible deadline. One year! Toyota executive Akihiro Wada told Uchiyamada, "Don't settle for anything less than a 100 percent improvement." Otherwise, Wada felt, Toyota's competitors—other auto manufacturers—would catch up too fast. "At that moment," Uchiyamada now recalls, "I felt he demanded too much."

Takeshi Uchiyamada was the chief engineer for the hybrid Toyota Prius project.

Sixteen-Hour Days

The team set to work, testing hundreds of engines. They worked sixteen hours a day, and tempers ran short. Sometimes fistfights broke out over design changes. They narrowed the design down to 80 options. Each time they came up with a new design, they tested it on the computer. They did a **computer simulation** to see how it would run. They narrowed those 80 down to 4 and then down to 1. They built a **prototype**. But the engine wouldn't start. "On the computer the hybrid power system worked very well," says chief power train engineer Satosi Ogiso. "But simulation is different from seeing if the actual part can work."

For a whole month, engineers worked to get the car to start! Then they finally had it, and in time for the Tokyo Motor Show. They called the car the Prius. (*Prius* comes from a Latin word meaning "before" or "ahead.") But then the real race began. Toyota had been planning to release the

The Toyota Prius is the result of many years of engine experimentation.

Prius in 1998. But Toyota's new president, Hiroshi Okuda, moved the date up a year. Now engineers had only two more years to finish all of their tests and solve any problems with the car. This meant that they had only two-thirds of the time it usually takes to develop an ordinary new car.

At first the model Prius did not work well. Once the car started, it would drive

only a few hundred yards. The battery would shut down if it got too hot or too cold. At one point, a team member had to sit in the passenger seat during road tests. The engineer in the passenger seat would monitor the car's temperature on a laptop computer. If the car got too hot, it would burst into flames. If it got too cold (below 14°F or –10°C) it would stop moving.

Slowly, engineers managed to correct each problem. The Prius's mileage crept up, finally reaching 66 miles (106.2km) per gallon. It also emitted 80 percent less air pollution than cars with traditional engines do.

While engineers worked with the engine, designers worked to come up with a plan for the car's body. Like the engineers, designers had to work around the clock to meet Toyota's deadlines. "Ordinarily we get two to three months to make sketches and prepare models," says Toyota designer Erwin Lui. "For the Prius, we got two to three weeks."

The long days paid off. Toyota finally released the Prius to the public in October 1997—two months ahead of schedule.

Hybrid Technology

What had Toyota's engineers done? They had designed a car that contains both a

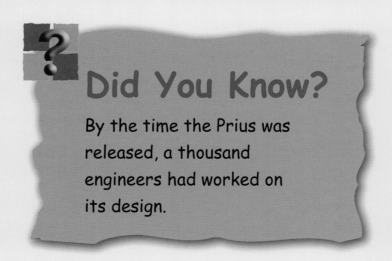

Did You Know?

By the time the Prius was released, a thousand engineers had worked on its design.

The Toyota hybrid engine combines a traditional gasoline engine with an electric battery.

gasoline engine and an electric battery. The car still uses gas but is so efficient that a little gas goes a long way. When the gasoline engine runs, it not only propels the car forward, it also charges the battery. When the battery is fully charged, the car can run on electric energy.

The Prius was also designed to capture the energy of braking. Normally, when a driver presses on a car's brake pedal, most of the energy of the car's movement forward is lost. But Toyota's engineers found a way to trap some of that energy and save it in the battery. They called the new system regenerative braking because the action of putting on the brakes could generate, or produce, energy. The energy collected in the braking process is regenerated—produced again—since it had already been produced once by the car's movement forward.

Uchiyamada and his team had beaten their deadline, and they had achieved something remarkable—a car that wasted less energy than any gasoline-burning car ever had. But would the new car sell? They weren't sure.

How Does Regenerative Braking Work?

The hybrid concept means that two things are combined in one. Hybrid cars combine a gasoline engine with an electric motor. But they also combine ordinary brakes with electric brakes.

In a gasoline-powered car, pressing the brake pedal causes brake pads to push against the wheels. Or it causes brake pads to press against a disc connected to the axle. The brake pads are like the brakes on a bicycle. They produce friction. This takes away some of the car's forward-moving energy, changing it to heat.

In a hybrid car, the car can use brake pads to slow down. If the car needs to slow down fast, it uses the brake pads. Then the energy is wasted. It becomes heat and disappears into the atmosphere. But if the driver applies the brake slowly, the car slows down in a different way. The onboard computer directs the electric motor to spin backward. This slows the car down gently. It also allows the electric motor to act like a generator. This means that it can produce electricity and store it in a battery. Later the car can use that energy to help it move forward. Or it can use the energy to give it a burst of speed.

The Prius first arrived in the United States in July of 2000. One Salt Lake City car dealer did not expect to sell many. "It was passable," he said. "It looked like it wouldn't embarrass us." The Prius turned out to be much more than "not an embarrassment." Within a few years it was changing the history of automaking.

Chapter 3

Changing the History of Automaking

The Prius was a remarkable invention and really met the goal to cut back on the use of gasoline made from fossil fuels. But people are funny. It can take them a long time to accept new ideas. Would Toyota be able to sell the Prius?

"I did not envisage . . . a major success at that time," remembers Toyota executive Katsuaki Watanabe. "Some thought it would grow rapidly, and others thought

Did You Know?

Toyota used to be known as a company that did not take risks. It was called a "fast follower." Toyota's strategy was to watch and wait while other companies took risks and then quickly catch up. With the Prius, Toyota executives broke their own rules. They threw caution to the wind and tried something new.

it would grow gradually. I was in the second camp."

The Prius did sell well in Japan, though. Toyota began producing 1,000 hybrid cars a month. But it soon had to double that number to meet the demand. The Prius had become known as a "green" car—a car that was better for the environment. Japanese buyers seemed proud to own a "green" car.

Even though the Prius sold well in Japan, Toyota executives worried about what would happen when their hybrid was introduced to the United States. The Prius had not sold well in China. Nor did it sell well in Europe. Toyota decided to release the car to the United States first in California. California's strict air pollution laws, they thought, would increase people's interest in buying a car that used less gasoline and emitted less air pollution. But they worried that American drivers would expect the car to come with an electric cord so they could plug it in, just like an electric car. This new model of the Prius could not be plugged into an outlet. Also, they knew that they would have to train car mechanics at automotive shops to fix the car and replace the parts. This might be a challenge for mechanics who were used to working only on traditional gasoline-engine cars.

Toyota shipped a few models of the Prius to California early. They invited interested buyers to come in for a test drive before the new cars arrived. The test drives did not go well. The test drive models were built to be used in Japan, so the steering wheels were on the right side

Mild Hybrids and True Hybrids

Racing to catch up with the Prius, some automakers had other ideas. They did not design new hybrid cars. Instead, they started with the gasoline cars they were already making. They replaced the gas engines with smaller engines. Then they added electric batteries. They also added an onboard computer to control the engine and the battery.

Hybrids that were designed this way are called "mild hybrids." They are still good at conserving fuel. They do not give off as much air pollution as ordinary cars do. And they can still convert some energy to battery power when the driver steps on the brakes. The Honda Insight, Chevrolet Malibu, and GM's Saturn Vue and Saturn Aura are all mild hybrids.

A "true hybrid," like the Toyota Prius or the Ford Escape, can do even more. It can drive at low speeds using just the electric motor. Driving with just the electric motor can startle some drivers. They may not notice that they have turned the car on, after turning the key in the ignition. The electric motor is very quiet compared to the gasoline engine. But true hybrids can drive without gasoline for short distances. On a fast-moving highway, though, hybrids also use their gas engines.

The Ford Escape, shown here, is a true hybrid. It uses the same technology as the Toyota Prius.

of the car, not the left. And some drivers were dismayed to find that a baby stroller would not fit in the car's trunk.

The Honda Insight

Even though buyers were skeptical at first, the Prius had already begun to change the history of automaking. Ever since Toyota introduced the first model Prius at the Tokyo Motor Show in 1995, Honda had been racing to catch up. Honda put together its own hybrid. It was a "mild hybrid," called the Insight. Honda began selling the Insight in the United States almost a year before Toyota was ready to ship the Prius to California.

Honda's engineers had worked hard to design the lightest, most efficient car they could. They used lightweight materials wherever possible. Much of the Insight is made of aluminum and plastic with rounded edges. This made the car very **aerodynamic**. They also chose to make the Insight a car that would appeal to single people living alone, not to families. They made the Insight a tiny, two-seat

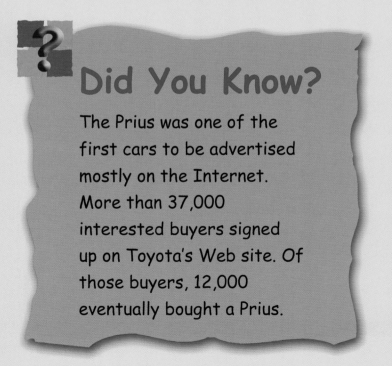

Did You Know?

The Prius was one of the first cars to be advertised mostly on the Internet. More than 37,000 interested buyers signed up on Toyota's Web site. Of those buyers, 12,000 eventually bought a Prius.

Honda began competing with Toyota for its share of the hybrid market when it came out with the Insight in 2000.

sports car. Journalist Greg Easterbrook described the new car: "Honda Insight . . . looks small enough to fit inside a standard minivan and come bursting out the way hidden supercars do in James Bond movies."

Although it was not a "true hybrid," Honda's strategy worked. The Insight got better mileage than the Prius. When the U.S. Environmental Protection Agency tested both cars, the Insight got 70 miles (112.6km) per gallon in highway driving. The Prius got 45 miles (72.4km) per gallon in highway driving. Honda also set up a 195-mile (313.82km) road trip contest. It invited automotive magazines to take the Insight on a trip and see who could get the best mileage. *Car and Driver Magazine* rigged up a large box on wheels. The box was towed by a Ford Excursion SUV. Inside the box, the magazine's technical editor drove the Honda Insight. The Insight was inches away from the SUV's bumper. But it was not connected to the SUV or the box in any way. The box simply protected the Insight from the wind. Without wind resistance, the Insight in the box got 121 miles (194.7km) out of a gallon of gas.

Arrival of the Prius

The Prius arrived in the United States in July 2000, seven months after the Insight. Gas prices, which were low when the Prius was first released, kept rising. American celebrities such as Leonardo DiCaprio, Cameron Diaz, Harrison Ford, and Calista Flockhart drove the Prius.

By 2003 owning a Prius had become a fashion statement. It was a way to show

From Mopeds to Submarines

Hybrid cars are not the only vehicles to get power from more than one source. Any type of vehicle that is powered in two or more ways can be called a hybrid. For example, a moped is a bicycle that can be pedaled but can also run on a gas motor. Diesel electric locomotives run on diesel fuel and electricity. Diesel is oil that has been processed into a heavier form than gasoline. It is more efficient but also causes more pollution than regular gasoline. Some cities, such as Seattle, have diesel-electric buses. Seattle chose to add hybrid buses to its fleet because its buses must sometimes drive through tunnels underground. While in the tunnels, the hybrid buses use only electric power. That way they do not pollute the tunnel air.

Submarines are also hybrid vehicles. A submarine can combine electric power with diesel fuel, nuclear power, or both. Nuclear submarines use nuclear reactors to generate electricity. The reactors are like the ones used at nuclear power plants. Nuclear reactors harness the energy that can be released by splitting an atom. Diesel submarines can only burn diesel fuel at the surface, where they can release the exhaust into the air. They must surface from time to time to run on diesel and charge up their electric batteries. But nuclear submarines can run nuclear reactors underwater. They can stay underwater for weeks at a time.

A General Motors hybrid bus drives its usual route. Hybrid engines are being put to use around the world.

Owning a Toyota Prius reflects a commitment toward helping save the environment.

one's commitment to the environment. People who wanted to buy a new car waited months for the second generation Prius. U.S. sales doubled in 2004 and nearly doubled again in 2005. Toyota executives changed their minds about this car that was supposed to lose money for years. Instead, Jim Press, president of Toyota's U.S. division, remarked, "It's the hottest car we've ever had."

Inspiring Other Automakers

By 2005 General Motors executives in Detroit, Michigan, were changing the way they thought about hybrids. After they saw the success of the Prius and the Insight, American automakers scrambled to develop their own hybrids. By 2008 every major automaker had come up with its own hybrid car. Most offered several hybrid options. Some were designed to save gas. Others do not save gas but just help the car to accelerate faster. Other options included making hybrid SUVs and minivans. These cars get worse gas mileage than traditional compact cars. But they get better mileage than nonhybrid SUVs and minivans.

In 2006 about 1.5 percent of all the cars and trucks sold in the United States were hybrids. (In all, 17 million cars and trucks were sold that year. About 250,000 of them were hybrids.) Hybrids are still hard to find in certain areas. Some companies sell them in states that they believe are very committed to environmentalism, like California or Colorado. So hybrids haven't changed the world yet. But they

Visitors at an auto show check out a cutaway of the Saturn SUV hybrid.

have rocked it. Automakers believe that hybrids will drop out of the market someday—when oil becomes truly scarce. But they also believe that hybrids are a necessary step. In the end, they hope to develop cars that will not rely on fossil fuels at all.

Chapter 4

What's Next?

In 2008 the auto industry was in crisis. Gas prices had reached record high levels. In some places gas cost over five dollars per gallon. Fewer people were buying cars. Car companies were losing money. In 2008 GM decided it could not afford to pay so many workers. The company planned to cut 74,000 workers from its payroll.

Planning for the Future

In 2008 less than 1 percent of new cars were hybrids or electric. Most cars and

Did You Know?

New cars today have more **electronics** than steel. They can communicate with satellites to tell a driver where the car is and how to get to another location. They can detect how close other cars are and parallel park themselves. They can automatically call for help in an emergency. Automakers expect someday to build a car that drives itself.

trucks still had gasoline engines. But many people felt that hybrid and electric technology would someday save the auto industry. Since the Prius was developed, every major car company has started working on hybrid and electric cars. But the technology was still very new. Car businesses were not sure which kind of car would be most practical. So they concentrated on two types of cars: plug-in hybrids and hydrogen cars.

Plug-In Cars

Hybrid cars use two sources of energy. But they do not use each source equally. The first wave of hybrids, like the Prius, relies mostly on gasoline. The electric motor mainly reduces the amount of gasoline the car uses. The next wave of hybrids, though, relies more on electricity and less on gas. These hybrids are electric cars. But they have a gas tank that can be used as a backup.

The old hybrids got their electricity from the gasoline engine. The engine would recharge the battery. Batteries were also recharged during the process of braking. The new hybrids are called "plug-ins." They can get their electricity from a wall socket. This means that owners can plug in their cars at night and have a fully charged battery in the morning. If they drive short distances, they might not have to use any gasoline at all.

Are plug-in cars really "green"? If owners get the electricity for their homes from coal-burning power plants, the car will still depend on fossil fuels. (Coal,

Toyota's new plug-in hybrid car, and its battery pack (inset), attract interest at an auto show.

through regenerative braking. And if a home is powered by a hydroelectric power plant or gets its electricity from its own solar power generator, the car could be free from fossil fuels. In 2008 most U.S. homes still got their electricity from coal-burning power plants. Still, many people hope that someday electricity will come mostly from renewable resources like solar, wind, and water power.

Why did Toyota not design a plug-in car the first time around? Batteries were a problem at first. Gasoline can store more energy in a smaller space than an ordinary battery can. Giving the car enough batteries to store energy for driving all the time

like oil, is a fossil fuel.) However, electric and hybrid cars do generate a small amount of electricity on their own,

How Plug-In Cars Work

Plug-in cars get their power mostly from electricity. The car can be plugged in at home overnight. It takes about six and a half hours to recharge. When the car begins to move, an electric motor powers the wheels. After the car has driven 40 miles (64.3km), the gasoline engine begins to work. But the gas engine does not power the wheels directly. Instead, the gas engine turns a generator to produce more electricity. The electricity goes to the electric motor and to the battery.

No matter where the electricity is coming from—the gas engine or the battery—the electric motor controls the wheels. The gas engine can also recharge the battery. It takes about 30 minutes of running the gas engine to recharge the battery. Then the car is ready to drive another 40 miles using just the battery again.

The Hybrid Car

- Battery Recharge Plug
- Electric Battery Pack
- Fuel Tank
- Power Electronics
- Electric Motor

Plug-in cars are part of the new wave in hybrid vehicles.

Did You Know?

Lithium ion battery fires are rare. Scientists say that they happen anywhere from one time in a million to one time in 10 million. Why do they happen at all? Lithium ion batteries are very sensitive to heat. If they get too hot, they overheat and catch fire. To make them safe for use in a car, engineers must find a way to protect the batteries from heat or to make them less sensitive to heat.

would mean adding extra weight. The extra weight would mean that the car would use more energy to move.

Now automakers have turned to a new technology—**lithium ion batteries**. Lithium ion batteries have been used for years in laptop computers and cell phones. They work well in laptops and phones because they are light. They also hold a charge for a long time. But carmakers were reluctant to use them in cars at first. Every now and then a lithium ion battery could burst into flames. For example, in 2006 a passenger on an airplane was carrying an extra lithium ion battery for a laptop. The battery caught fire in a carry-on bag stowed in one of the plane's overhead compartments. Flight attendants quickly put out the fire with a fire extinguisher. But in a car, a sudden battery fire could cause a tragic accident.

Now automakers are able to sell cars that use the lithium ion technology. Honda, however, has held out. The president of Honda, Takeo Fukui, says that he prefers a different technology—hydrogen cars.

Hydrogen Fuel Cells

Honda released its first **hydrogen vehicle,** the FCX Clarity, in 2008. Hydrogen cars carry hydrogen in their fuel tanks. They combine the hydrogen with oxygen from the air to make water vapor. Water is made of hydrogen and oxygen. The process of making water vapor also produces electricity. So a hydrogen car is still an electric car. But it is an electric car that gets its electricity from a different source.

Hydrogen's use is exciting. First, like other electric cars, hydrogen cars do not emit pollutants. They do give out water vapor. Water vapor is safe for people to breathe. For this reason, hydrogen cars are considered **zero emission vehicles**.

Lithium ion batteries, like the one shown here, hold a charge for a long time.

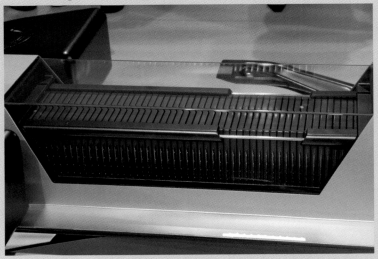

(Top) Japanese automaker Honda expects to mass produce its hydrogen vehicle, the FCX Clarity. (Bottom) To solve the problem of fueling a hydrogen vehicle, Honda has come up with the Home Energy Station. This system removes hydrogen from natural gas.

Second, hydrogen cars can drive much farther than lithium ion plug-ins. The Clarity can drive 270 miles (434.5km) before it needs more fuel.

Hydrogen technology has its drawbacks, though. Once a car does run out of fuel, it needs a place to fuel up.

Honda has another solution to the fueling problem—a Home Energy Station. The Home Energy Station takes hydrogen out of natural gas. Many homes are already connected to natural gas lines because they use it for their heating and cooking. The Home Energy Station can take hydrogen from gas lines and refill the Clarity's tank in three to five minutes. It takes another day to store up enough hydrogen to refill the Clarity again. At the same time, the Home Energy Station can produce electricity, heat, and hot water for the home. The Home Energy Station is exciting, but it still relies on a fossil fuel—natural gas. However, natural gas burns more cleanly than oil and coal do.

Like lithium ion technology, hydrogen fuel seems promising to automakers. Most have developed hydrogen cars as well as lithium ion plug-ins. Ford has produced a fleet of hydrogen shuttle buses. They are used in airports to carry people to and from the parking garages. Daimler-Chrysler made several hydrogen buses for Iceland. (Iceland also has a hydrogen refueling station and a handful of hydrogen test cars.)

Compressed Air Technology

Plug-in cars and hydrogen cars are both types of electric cars. But some engineers have found a better way to generate electricity for a car. Why rely on fossil fuels, they say, when you can build a car that runs on air? French engineer Guy Negre has invented a car that runs on the same kind of air you probably use to pump up your bicycle tires. His car is called the Air Car. Like hydrogen cars, the Air Car is a zero emissions vehicle. It uses only air, which is available everywhere. And its only byproduct is air.

Air Car designer Guy Negre shows how his compressed-air engine works.

How can a car run on air? **Compressed air** can be used to generate electricity. First, the air is stored under high pressure. The pressure forces a lot of air to remain in a small space. Air that is not under pressure will expand to fill a larger space. So when the air is let out of the tank, the expanding air can be used to turn a **turbine**. It works like a windmill.

Many gas stations already have air compressors, which customers can use to add air to their tires. These air compressors are the same ones that you might use to fill a bicycle's tires. Using a gas station's air compressor, an Air Car driver can fill his or her tank in about three minutes. The cost of a tank of air is about two dollars. The Air Car can drive 125 miles (201.1km) on a tank of air. It can reach speeds of up to 70 miles (112.6km) per hour.

India's Tata Motors began selling the Air Car in 2008. Tata added a gasoline engine to the car. That way drivers are able to use the car for long trips between gas stations.

Today many people feel that the automobile industry is at a crossroads. People will,

The Car of the Future—Not

New car designs are often inspired by new technologies in other areas. In the 1950s jet planes were a new technology. They inspired GM's experimental car, the XP-21 Firebird. GM hoped to build a car that would look and drive like a jet. It did. The Firebird could hit 100 miles (160.9km) per hour easily. The engine could make the car go even faster, but at those speeds the wheels broke loose from the car in test drives.

How did the Firebird work? Jet planes use turbine engines. First they burn a fuel. The heat from the burning fuel causes air to expand. The rapidly expanding air pushes the blades of a turbine around. It works like a windmill, similar to the turbine that is used in the Air Car today. However, the Air Car's turbine generates electricity. The turbine engine did not generate electricity. It powered the car directly.

Whatever happened to the XP-21? GM never sold it. It was used only as an experimental car. From the Firebird, GM learned how to make a car's ride smoother and how to improve the brakes.

GM's XP-21 Firebird looked like a jet and even drove like one, but it never sold.

Did You Know?

The first Air Cars were made of fiberglass, not steel. The body for the car is glued together, not welded. They may not sound very high-tech—but they come with a computer and a wireless Internet connection. And an Air Car driver doesn't use a key. Instead, he or she unlocks the car with an access card.

slowly, have to stop using transportation that gets its energy from fossil fuel. But no one is sure what technology will be the best choice to take its place. Millions of people already own cars that have gasoline engines. Gasoline cars, hybrid cars, and electric cars will have to share the roads for some years to come. At some point, though, the tide will turn. If your grandchildren want to see what an old-fashioned gasoline car is like, they may have to find one in a museum.

Glossary

aerodynamic: Offering less resistance to air or wind.

compressed air: Air that has been pushed, or pressed, into a small space.

computer simulation: A test of how changing one or more variables in a car's design may affect its performance. In a computer simulation the test only takes place in the computer's program, not in the real world.

electric cars: Cars that run on electricity.

electronics: Parts of a car that use electricity, such as computers and sound systems.

fossil fuel: Fuel formed from the remains of dead plants and animals that lived millions of years ago. Because fossil fuels take millions of years to form, they are considered nonrenewable resources.

fuel efficiency: The ability to make the best use of the fuel being used.

hybrid: A car that uses two or more types of energy, such as gasoline and electricity.

hydrogen vehicle: A vehicle that runs on electricity that has been generated by combining hydrogen and oxygen to make water.

lithium ion batteries: Batteries made of lithium. These batteries can hold their charge for long periods of time and are very lightweight.

mileage: The distance a car can drive using a gallon of gas.

oil shale: A type of rock that has oil in its pores.

politics: The process of governing a country.

prototype: A model; a car that shows what an automaker plans to make. Finished cars are often very different from the original prototypes.

recharge: To add more energy to a battery.

refined: The removal of dirt and other unwanted particles.

reserves: An area of land set aside for a certain purpose, in this case for drilling oil.

turbine: A machine that converts the power of a moving substance (such as water or air) to electric power.

zero emission vehicles: Cars or trucks that do not give off any pollutants.

For More Information

Books

Ulrich Bethscheider-keiser, *Green-Designed Future Cars: Hybrid, Electrical, Bio-fuel Cell*. Hamburg, Germany: Avedition, 2008. Includes more information on different types of green cars.

Sherry Boschert, *Plug-In Hybrids: The Cars That Will Recharge America*. Gabriola Island, British Columbia: New Society, 2006. Makes an argument that plug-in cars will be ready for the general public sooner than hydrogen vehicles will be.

Karen Povey, *Our Environment: Hybrid Cars*. Farmington Hills, MI: KidHaven, 2006. Explains how hybrid cars work and what impact they might have on the environment.

Niki Walker, *Energy Revolution: Hydrogen: Running on Water*. New York: Crabtree, 2007. Explains how hydrogen power works and what forms of energy it can replace.

Web Sites

Alternative Power: Propulsion After Petroleum, Petersen Automotive Museum (www.petersen.org/default.cfm?docid=1043). A history of car design, including the earliest hybrid cars. Includes photos.

History of Electric Cars, Alfred P. Sloane Foundation, Stanford University (http://sloan.stanford.edu/EVonline/welcome.htm). A Web site devoted to the history of electric cars. Includes a "Drivers Tell All" section in which electric car users tell their stories. Some drivers also tell how they converted gasoline-powered cars to make them into electric vehicles.

HowStuffWorks (www.howstuffworks.com). A Web site devoted to explaining technology step by step. Includes articles on how electric cars, hybrid cars, fuel cells, and lithium ion batteries work.

U.S. Environmental Protection Agency, Department of Energy (www.fuel economy.gov). A Web site devoted to comparing the fuel economy of different cars. Includes a calculator that compares the miles per gallon of different brands and makes of cars, allowing users to look up a car by year, make, and model. The calculator provides a carbon footprint score and an air pollution score for each car, along with an estimation of how many barrels of oil that car uses per year (based on average use).

Index

Accord (Honda), 10
Air Car, 39–40, 42
Aleklett, Kjell, 7

Batteries, 36-37
Buses
  hybrid, 27
  hydrogen, 39

Car and Driver Magazine, 26
Caroline Electric Vehicle
  Coalition (CEVC), 11
Compressed air technology, 39
Corolla (Toyota), 14

DaimlerChrysler, 39

Easterbrook, Greg, 26
Ecostar (Ford), 12
Electric cars
  disadvantages of, 12
  early, 8–9
  plug-in, 33–34, 35
Electricity, 34
Electronics, 32
Environmental Protection
  Agency (EPA), 26

EV1 (General Motors), 12

F.A. Woods Auto Company, 15
Ford Motor Company, 10, 11,
  39
Fukui, Takeo, 37

Gasoline, 5
Gasoline shortage, of 1970s,
  4–5, 10
General Motors, 29, 32
  turbine engine car of, 41
Geo Metro, 10

Home Energy Station, 39
Honda, 24–26
  hydrogen vehicle developed
  by, 37
Hybrid cars
  early, 15
  mild vs. true, 23
  plug-in, 33–34, 35
  technology of, 18–19
  Toyota's work on, 14, 16–18
Hydrogen fuel cells, 37–39

Inflation, 8

Insight (Honda), 24–26

Kimbara, Yoshiro, 14

Lithium ion batteries, 36–37

Minivans, 29

Negre, Guy, 39

Ogiso, Satosi, 17
Oil
  amount used daily, 13
  formation of, 6
  is a scarce resource, 5–6
Oil reserves, 7
Oil shale, 6

Plug-in cars, 33–35
Porsche, Ferdinand, 15
Press, Jim, 29
Prius (Toyota), 17–19, 28
  as inspiration, 29
  introduction to U.S., 22, 24,
  26, 29

Ranger pickup (Ford), 12

Regenerative breaking, 19, 20

SMARTT (Students Making
  Advancements in Renewable
  Technology), 11
Solectria Corporation, 10
Submarines, 27
SUVs, 13, 29

Tata Motors, 40
Toyoda, Eiji, 13
Toyota, 21
  fuel-efficient car of, 14, 16–
  18
  hybrid technology developed
  by, 18–20
Turbine engines, 41

Uchiyamada, Takeshi, 14, 16,
  19
U.S. Electricar, 10

Wada, Akihiro, 16
Watanabe, Katsuaki, 21–22

XP-21 Firebird (experimental
  car), 41

Picture Credits

Cover: Associated Press
AFP/Getty Images, 19, 40
Associated Press, 5, 11, 16, 25, 27
© Car Culture/Corbis, 15
Daniel Lippitt/AFP/Getty Images, 17
Danny Moloshok/Reuters/Landov, 38 (bottom)
Getty Images, 41
Kimberly White/Reuters/Landov, 34 (bottom)
Kimimasa Mayama/Bloomberg News /Landov, 38 (top)

Jeffrey Sauger/Bloomberg News/Landov, 28
© Mark Scheuern/Alamy, 37
North Wind Picture Archives/Alamy, 9
Robert Gilhooly/Bloomberg News/Landov, 34 (top)
Steve Fecht/UPI/Landov, 30-31
Steve Zmina, 35
Tina Manley/News/Alamy, 10
© Transtock Inc./Alamy, 23

About the Author

Bonnie Juettner is a writer and editor of children's reference books and educational videos and a mother of two. She currently drives a Toyota Corolla but hopes someday to drive a hybrid or an electric car.